Writing with the Seasons

52 creative prompts
inspired by nature's rhythms

Gabrielle Ariella Kaplan-Mayer

Smith Street Books

Introduction

Welcome to *Writing with the Seasons*!

This journal invites you to explore the spiraling cycles of life and the rhythm of the natural world through 52 expressive writing prompts. Each prompt helps you connect your inner world of insight and intuition with the ever-changing landscapes around you.

Writing with the Seasons is grounded in three key ideas:

- Humans are part of, not separate from, the natural world.
- Each of us is inherently creative in our own unique way.
- Our everyday lives hold countless opportunities for experiencing the profound.

The journal is divided into four sections, one for each season. Each of the 12 seasonal weekly themes offers a unique topic to spark your imagination through:

- a meditative introduction inviting you to set intentions for the week ahead
- a connection to signs and symbols that illuminate the theme
- inspiration from a poet, writer or philosopher
- a simple meditative or reflective practice.

Then, the seasonal reflection at the end of each section offers a chance to reflect on what has passed, and what wisdom you are carrying forward as you approach a new season.

You can move through the journal chronologically or follow your own rhythm. Begin wherever you find yourself—in any season of the year or of your life. You might choose a theme that mirrors your current energy, or simply open to a random page and see what calls to you. There are no rules here—only invitations.

Whether you live where the seasons shift dramatically or in a place where the landscape remains steady, whether your home is a high-rise apartment, a farmhouse, in a suburban neighborhood or a small quiet town, *Writing with the Seasons* offers ways to strengthen your connection with both the natural world and your own imagination.

Each season offers a beautiful metaphor for our inner lives. Each season carries its own qualities and energy—times of growth, stillness, release, and renewal—that we, too, experience within ourselves.

Science continues to affirm what many writers have long known: expressive writing can be deeply healing. Just 15 or 20 minutes of reflection each week can bring solace, clarity, and inspiration. So, settle in with a warm coffee or a cool tea—depending on the season—and begin.

To life. To creativity. To the turning of the seasons—inside and around us.

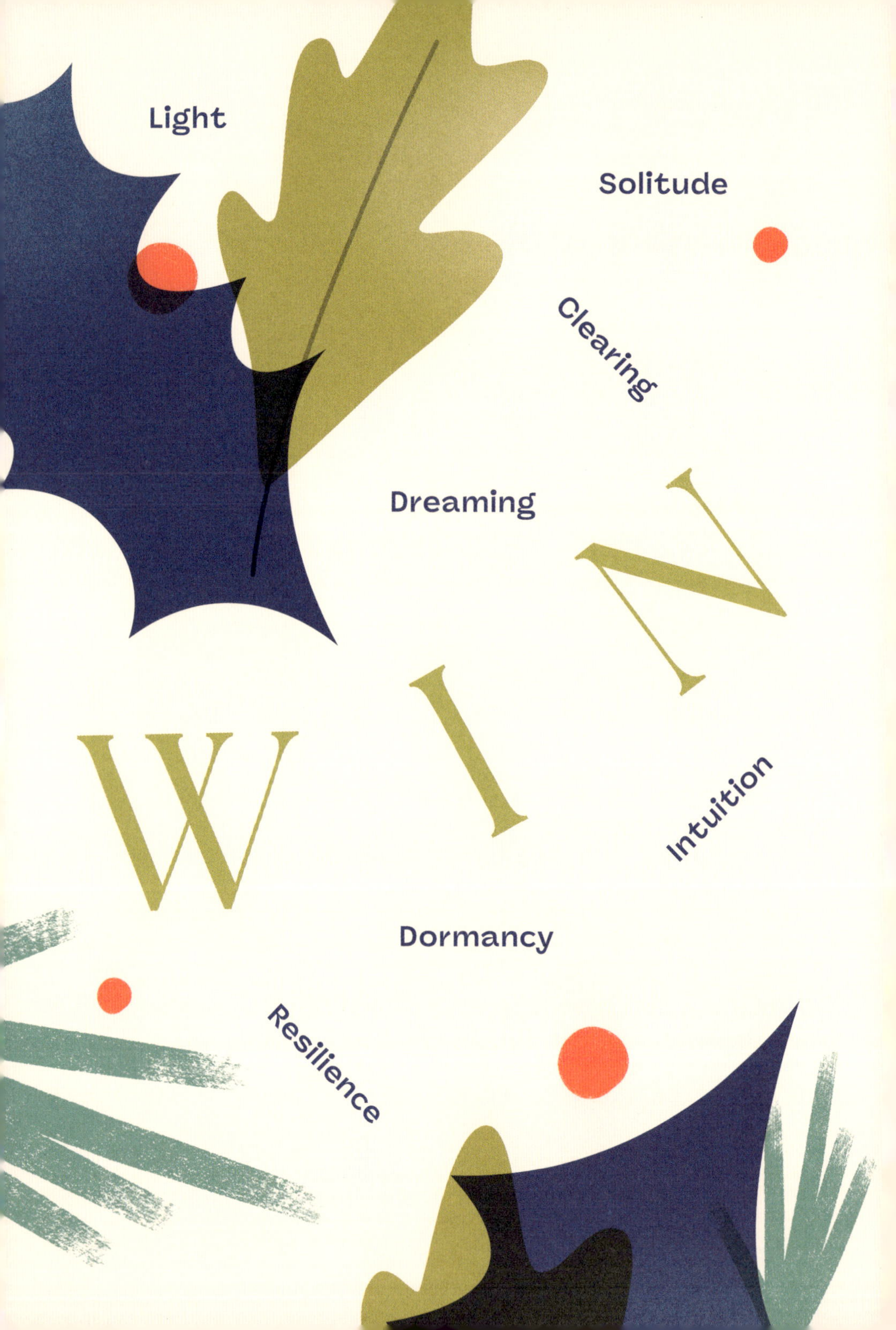
Light
Solitude
Clearing
Dreaming
W I N
Intuition
Dormancy
Resilience

Glimmers

Peace

T E R

Stillness

Hope

Rejuvenation

During the winter months, as many plants and animals hibernate and the outer world lies still, we too are invited to turn inward. Winter holds a quiet beauty—a season of peace, rest, and renewal. It also offers the opportunity to experience cold weather fully, to feel its sharpness and learn how our bodies adapt to the chill. In winter's stillness, we can uncover our own calm and notice the gentle glimmer of hope for new life beginning to stir beneath the surface.

These prompts are designed to help you move through winter in harmony with your dreams and inner resilience. You can return to them anytime, in any season—whenever you long for the beauty of cold winter nights, connection to your intuition, or time to dream.

Weekly theme

Light

Setting intentions

The winter solstice, which was traditionally celebrated with bonfires and festive gatherings, marks the longest night of the year. Though the start of winter feels like a dark time, after solstice night, daylight begins to gradually increase.

Write/draw/doodle your hopes and intentions for the week ahead. Consider ways you might bring more light—literal or metaphorical—into your week.

Some prompts to spark your reflections

I feel a sense of light around me when ...
The light I'm seeking is ...
When the world feels dark, I can ...

Date: / /

Searching for signs and symbols

Notice where the theme of *light* shows up this week in your dreams, landscape, or imagination. Winter holidays from across traditions invoke light as a symbol of divine presence, hope, and connection. Is there a particular symbol of light that speaks to you?

Write/draw/doodle about the light *connections that you find around you.*

What fire could
ever equal the sunshine
of a winter's day ...
The warmth comes directly
from the sun, and is not
radiated from the earth,
as in summer; and when
we feel his beams
on our backs ... we are
grateful as for a special
kindness, and bless the sun
which has followed us
into that by-place.

Henry David Thoreau

Embracing mindfulness

When sunlight arrives in winter it can fill us with gratitude and hope. Even on dark and cold days, you can actively imagine the sun's light surrounding you. Call on that sunlight whenever you need it!

Weekly practice

The start of the season is an ideal time to plan for how to bring more light into your home through candles, lamps, or other sources—and to plan for activities, including writing in this journal, that can increase your inner light and energy. The winter sun comes from a lower angle, which allows for vibrant sunsets. Go outside and experience the sun setting as often as you can.

Weekly theme

Solitude

Setting intentions

Just as some animals hibernate in winter, this can also be a season when humans feel a natural inclination for solitude. With shorter days and longer nights, winter is an ideal time to reach deep into our inner lives.

Write/draw/doodle your hopes and intentions for the week ahead. Consider ways you might slow down and find little moments for solitude this week. What benefits do you discover when you make time to turn inward?

Some prompts to spark your reflections

When I am alone, I discover ...

Moments of solitude offer me ...

Entering the week, I wish for ...

Date: / /

Searching for signs and symbols

Notice where the theme of *solitude* shows up this week in your dreams, landscape, or imagination. Are there solitary animals you connect to? Or special places nearby where you find solitary space?

Write/draw/doodle about the solitude *connections that you find around you.*

Loneliness is
the poverty of self;
solitude is richness
of self.

May Sarton

Embracing mindfulness

What do you appreciate about the "richness of self"? What is your preferred balance of time in solitude and time with others?

Weekly practice

Think of solitude as an art, a creative practice. Choose a simple activity, like making a cup of tea, taking a wintry walk outdoors, or drawing a bath and give yourself 15 to 30 minutes once or twice during the week simply to be with your spirit. Turn ringers off, put away devices and see what happens.

Weekly theme

Clearing

Setting intentions

In winter, we sense nature's stillness. If we were to step into a clearing in the forest, we'd be surrounded by barren trees and could better see the horizon. The metaphor of clearing invites us to use winter as a time to remove unwanted physical or emotional elements in our lives that no longer serve us.

Write/draw/doodle your hopes and intentions for the week ahead. Consider what kinds of things you're ready to clear: old behaviors, objects, or energy that can be let go.

Some prompts to spark your reflections

I'm ready to let go of ...
It's safe to clear away ...
I release and welcome in ...

Date: / /

Searching for signs and symbols

Notice where the theme of *clearing* shows up this week in your dreams, landscape, or imagination. Spend time with a leafless tree and notice its beauty. Walk through a snowy meadow or field, along the seashore, around a lake's perimeter, or along any clear space near you. See what it might communicate to you.

Write/draw/doodle about the clearing *connections that you find around you.*

I see the clearing
in the wood
where the soul
may breathe.

Unknown

Embracing mindfulness

How do clear spaces make you feel? Think about clear spaces in nature and also other peaceful places like galleries, meditation studios, or locations where your soul has space to breathe.

Weekly practice

Our minds, routines, and spaces can become cluttered in ways that we don't even notice. It takes intention to look at what's around and inside of us that we no longer need. Be gentle with yourself as you move through your week with clearing eyes. You might reach out to a friend and support each other with inner and outer clearing.

Weekly theme

Dreaming

Setting intentions

Because winter offers us more dark hours, it's an ideal time to tune into dreaming—by journaling about our dreams, and also paying attention to daydreams and moments of imagination. Dreams provide us with a different kind of information from what our waking mind perceives.

Write/draw/doodle your hopes and intentions for the week ahead. Bring in any recent dreams or daydreams. Think about ways you can get cozy and settle into the evening to open yourself up to deep sleep and remembering dreams.

Some prompts to spark your reflections

With the darker nights ...

I open myself to dreaming when ...

My dreams tell me that ...

Date: / /

Searching for signs and symbols

Notice where the theme of *dreaming* shows up this week in your own dreams, landscape, or imagination. Don't worry if you don't have a particularly memorable dream this week. Just having dreams on your mind might bring back an image or fragment from a memorable dream from your past.

Write/draw/doodle about the dreaming *connections that you find around you.*

Every great dream begins with a dreamer.

Harriet Tubman

Embracing mindfulness

There may be things you're dreaming of that you haven't spoken about to anyone. This journal is a place where you can write them, reflect on them, and give them space to come to life!

Weekly practice

Make your bedtime routine relaxed and cozy. Take time for a warm bath before bed, a cup of chamomile or other soothing tea, play music that you like. When we ease into sleep, it can help to open our dreams.

Weekly theme

Dormancy

Setting intentions

Many types of plants become dormant during the colder weather—it's a survival mechanism to conserve energy. Dormancy can also relate to humans when we're in a state of being temporarily inactive. Many people feel lower energy during the cold, dark months of winter and rather than resisting that state, you could embrace the ways that winter can be a wonderfully slower time.

Write/draw/doodle your hopes and intentions for the week ahead. Consider how you can be gentle with yourself and allow life to move at a softer, slower pace.

Some prompts to spark your reflections

I allow myself to slow down by ...

I am not obligated to ...

More and more, I understand that moving slower can ...

Date: / /

Searching for signs and symbols

Notice where the theme of *dormancy* shows up this week in your dreams, landscape, or imagination. From bears to bumblebees, squirrels to skunks, a number of animals hibernate through the winter; mythology around them can spark our imaginations.

Write/draw/doodle about the dormancy *connections that you find around you.*

Nature looks dead in winter because her life is gathered into her heart.

Hugh Macmillan

Embracing mindfulness

When we observe nature's cycles, we're reminded that humans are part of nature, not separate from it. Winter does not need to be a time of ending, but a gentle pause before the renewal of spring.

Weekly practice

Humans don't need the same kind of rest that certain animals and elements in nature need during the winter months, but each of us needs some restorative time. If you normally feel overscheduled, look at your calendar and block out times for restful activities. Notice how you feel when you take more time for rest.

Weekly theme

Intuition

Setting intentions

Intuition is a kind of understanding that arises instantly—a knowing that comes from a place beyond reason. Winter's darker days, cold weather, and quiet stillness draw us inward, where our intuitive sense can grow stronger.

Write/draw/doodle your hopes and intentions for the week ahead. Reflect on the role intuition plays in your life. Do you notice your intuition becoming clearer during the winter months?

Some prompts to spark your reflections

I have been sensing that ...
My sense of intuition offers me ...
Entering the week, I wish for ...

Date: / /

Searching for signs and symbols

Notice where the theme of *intuition* shows up this week in your dreams, landscape, or imagination. Snow, owls, fairies, and other winter elements carry deep symbolism connected to inner wisdom.

Write/draw/doodle about the intuition *connections that you find around you.*

Trust thyself:
every heart vibrates
to that iron string.

Ralph Waldo Emerson

Embracing mindfulness

Strengthening intuition begins with self-trust. That trust lives not only in your mind but also in your body. Pay attention to sensations and feelings that arise—they are often your intuition speaking.

Weekly practice

Reflecting on intuitive insights helps you recognize and deepen them. This week, notice moments when your intuition stirs, and record them in your journal. What messages might your intuition be offering you?

Weekly theme

Resilience

Setting intentions

Resilience is the capacity to withstand and recover from difficulties. Our ancestors needed resilience to survive the winter months, stretching their dried and stored food to last through the dark and cold. Today, we may not face the same physical hardships, but many of us still struggle with a kind of cabin fever that comes from spending more time indoors. We can call on our own resilience to help us experience these long winter nights with strength—and even joy.

Write/draw/doodle your hopes and intentions for the week ahead. Reflect on what helps you find strength during tough moments. What new kinds of inner resilience have you discovered this season?

Some prompts to spark your reflections
I am able to adapt by ...
When faced with challenges, I can ...
If difficulties arise, I might ...

Date: / /

Searching for signs and symbols

Notice where the theme of *resilience* shows up this week in your dreams, landscape, or imagination. People who have risen above immense challenges often become symbols of resilience: Think about Frederick Douglass, Malala Yousafzai, Helen Keller, Nelson Mandela, Frida Kahlo, Harvey Milk, and many others. A resilient figure you feel connected to may have an important lesson to teach you.

Write/draw/doodle about the resilience *connections that you find around you.*

With the new day comes new strength and new thoughts.

Eleanor Roosevelt

Embracing mindfulness

Some days, we simply can't find our resilience—and that's okay. On those days, practice self-care and compassion. Trust that a new day will come, bringing fresh strength and renewed perspective.

Weekly practice

Just like you might train for a marathon or to increase your strength in any area, resilience is a tool that can be built up with practice. Gratitude increases resilience—and so does journaling! Your commitment to 52 weeks of mindful journaling will strengthen your resilience through the seasons. As you write in the journal this week, remember that you're building resilience. If it's hard to find time for journaling, allocate time in your calendar and set a reminder so you have time to build your resilience scheduled into your week.

Weekly theme

Glimmers

Setting intentions

Glimmers are micro-moments that spark peace or contentment. They can be simple, daily experiences that remind us that life can be joyful. Through the winter months, the natural world offers us a multitude of glimmers: seeing a red cardinal in a snow-covered tree, catching the vibrant sunset lighting up the sky, hearing the wind rustle through trees. Noticing glimmers can keep our spirits strong.

Write/draw/doodle your hopes and intentions for the week ahead. Think about the kinds of things in the natural world that evoke positive feelings for you. If you enjoy sunrises or sunsets, make time to get outside and experience them. When you pay attention to glimmer moments, more of them tend to appear!

Some prompts to spark your reflections

Some things that make me feel peaceful are ...
I feel joyful when ...
These glimmers all around me are ...

Date: / /

Searching for signs and symbols

Notice where the theme of *glimmers* shows up this week in your dreams, landscape, or imagination. Bring all of your senses into the experience of glimmers. They could come from scents and aromas—especially cozy ones in winter months like cinnamon, pine, and citrus that can energize our spirits.

Write/draw/doodle about the glimmer *connections that you find around you.*

Only when it is dark enough can you see the stars.

Martin Luther King Jr.

Embracing mindfulness

In the dark and cold of winter, it can be hard to notice the beauty around us. If it's cold where you are, bundle up and spend some time outdoors, looking for beautiful things.

Weekly practice

Finding glimmers can be contagious in the best possible way! When you see something that sparks joy or peace, snap a picture or jot down some words or scribbles about it. Maybe you spot the first flower on a plant, catch your cat in an especially cuddly moment, or feel the bright winter sun coming through your window. Share with a friend and invite them to send you their "glimmer of the day." You can be "glimmer accountability" buddies and increase your appreciation of wonderful things together.

Weekly theme

Stillness

Setting intentions

We live in a culture that encourages us to always be doing—to be productive. Stillness is just the opposite; it invites us to pause for calm, quiet, and serenity. Winter is a season of conserving energy—the hours of darkness are longer, and many of us crave more sleep. This makes winter the ideal time for a natural slowdown from constant activity so we can simply be.

Write/draw/doodle your hopes and intentions for the week ahead. Think about ways that you can slow down this week and not take on extra activities or responsibilities. How does it feel to nurture yourself rather than expect yourself to do more?

Some prompts to spark your reflections

I can slow down by ...
More and more, I am seeing ways that ...
I notice a sense of stillness inside me when ...

Date: / /

Searching for signs and symbols

Notice where the theme of *stillness* shows up this week in your dreams, landscape, or imagination. If you have an embodied practice like yoga, tai chi, or Qi Gong, you might think about how your body feels when still during those practices.

Write/draw/doodle about the stillness *connections that you find around you.*

Heard melodies
are sweet, but
those unheard
Are sweeter ...

John Keats

Embracing mindfulness

Silence can be inviting but also frightening when we're not used to listening to it. Try short periods of silence this week—even five or ten minutes at a time—and notice the music in silence and stillness.

Weekly practice

The world won't wait for us to be still, but we can insist on time for quiet and calm. This week, put some time in your calendar for mindful outdoor excursions. Bundle up and take a slow, mindful walk. Or you might set up a bird feeder near a window, put out birdseed, and quietly wait to observe the birds who come to eat there.

Weekly theme

Peace

Setting intentions

The winter season—with its quiet, stillness, and cozy moments—naturally evokes a sense of peace. When we draw our energy inward during these colder months, we create space for peaceful feelings.

Write/draw/doodle your hopes and intentions for the week ahead. Reflect on where and when you find a sense of inner peace, and how you might deepen that feeling in your daily life.

Some prompts to spark your reflections

Peace comes when ...

I welcome peace by ...

Entering the week, I can turn inward by ...

Date: / /

Searching for signs and symbols

Notice where the theme of *peace* shows up this week in your dreams, landscape, or imagination. Look outdoors for natural signs that evoke peace: the hush of snowfall, the calm of bare trees, or the gentle rhythm of your own breathing. Listen to music that soothes you and stay open to unexpected moments of calm.

Write/draw/doodle about the peace *connections that you find around you.*

No winter lasts forever, no spring skips its turn.

Hal Borland

Embracing mindfulness

Part of what brings a sense of peace in winter is trust—trusting that the seasons will turn and new life will emerge. When we carry that same trust within ourselves, peace naturally takes root inside us.

Weekly practice

We don't have to wait to get away to a spa or retreat center to cultivate peace in our environment. Create a sense of calm and peace in your living environment by bringing in plants, setting up a quiet corner for meditation or prayer, or even paint a room a calming color. Notice how your inner sense of peace shifts when you've created a more peaceful living space.

Weekly theme

Hope

Setting intentions

Hope is a feeling of trust in what will come. During the winter months, we can foster hope by remembering nature's cycles—that spring always follows winter. The darker months can be a time for visualizing and actively imagining what we desire. We can look at plants and trees that may look barren but contain within them seeds of new life waiting to open.

Write/draw/doodle your hopes and intentions for the week ahead. Consider ways you might look for hopeful things and encourage hopeful thinking through the week. What helps you to feel trust when doubts—which are natural—arise?

Some prompts to spark your reflections

I feel trust in ...

On darker days, I can ...

More and more, I find hope when ...

Date: / /

Searching for signs and symbols

Notice where the theme of *hope* shows up this week in your dreams, landscape, or imagination. The dove is probably the best known symbol of hope, but across world mythologies, hope is represented in different forms. You might also imagine hope contained in the quiet earth, or nesting flower bulbs ready to sprout with color.

Write/draw/doodle about the hope *connections that you find around you.*

Hope is the thing with feathers
That perches in the soul,
And sings the tune without the words,
And never stops at all ...

Emily Dickinson

Embracing mindfulness

What do you imagine when you hear Emily Dickinson's vision of hope as a "thing with feathers"? How does that resemble (or not) your sense of how hope feels?

Weekly practice

We all have moments when hope feels far away. Go through your writing in this journal so far and put a sticky note or bookmark on pages where you express a hopeful sentiment. That way, you can return to read it on a day when hope feels far away. Sometimes, we can be our own best teachers!

Weekly theme

Rejuvenation

Setting intentions

Rejuvenation refers to the state of being restored. When we think of our own mental, physical, and emotional energy, we know what it feels like to be depleted and what it's like to be full of life. During the winter months, it may look like the natural world is in a state of decline, but when we look under the surface at the roots and trees, we know that new life is preparing to emerge in the spring. That pattern can be a model for us to follow, too.

Write/draw/doodle your hopes and intentions for the week ahead. Consider how you might restore your energy in small daily ways. What gives you vitality and vigor?

Some prompts to spark your reflections

I feel energized when ...

I can restore my spirit by ...

More and more, I am mindful that ...

Date: / /

Searching for signs and symbols
Notice where the theme of *rejuvenation* shows up this week in your dreams, landscape, or imagination. Look for signs of life returning in nature, like emerging flowers, returning birds, and fresher air.

Write/draw/doodle about the rejuvenation *connections that you find around you.*

Laughter is the sun that drives winter from the human face.

Victor Hugo

Embracing mindfulness

What do you turn to when your heart/mind/spirit is feeling weary? Think of a time when you felt rejuvenated; let yourself experience that memory and notice how your energy shifts.

Weekly practice

Sometimes breaking up routines can restore our energy. This week, try engaging in a new activity—which could be as simple as heading outside for stargazing in the evening, bundling up and taking a short night walk, or even walking a different trail. Disrupting patterns can go far in disrupting winter doldrums!

Winter reflections

When we pay attention to seasonal transitions, they can become powerful gateways to new adventures and opportunities. Take a moment to reflect on the peace, resilience, rejuvenation, and glimmers that you experienced this winter. You may also want to acknowledge any challenges or grief that shaped these past months. Write down the insights and wisdom you've gathered—gifts that can enrich your life as you step into spring.

Make this reflection page as interactive and personal as you like! You might paste in a ticket stub from a favorite film, play, or winter concert; a favorite winter recipe; a photo or two; even some pine needles or other items collected on a nature walk.

Some prompts to spark your reflections

Favorite people I shared time with ...
Beautiful places I experienced ...
New and enjoyable activities ...
Times when I felt vibrant, connected, alive ...
All that I hope to release ...
Wisdom I'm carrying into the new season ...

Awakening
Planting seeds
S P R
Dawn
Cleansing
Sunshine
Honoring earth
Festivity

Springtime is the season of awakening. Flowers bloom, trees bud, and animals emerge full of life and energy. As the sunlight grows stronger, we're also drawn outdoors—reconnecting with one another and with the natural world. It's a time for planting seeds that will take root and grow into summer's abundance.

In harmony with nature's rhythm, we can shake off winter's quiet, join in the happiness of seasonal festivities, and feel the vitality of new life all around us.

These prompts are designed to help you move through spring with awareness of its beauty and energy. You can return to them anytime, in any season—whenever you long for sunshine, new beginnings, and a deeper connection to the earth.

Energy

Connection

Beauty

Embodiment

Joy

Weekly theme

Awakening

Setting intentions

Spring is the season of rebirth—of the landscape coming back to life in magical ways, with trees that were bare all winter sprouting leaves and buds, flowers emerging from the earth, migrating birds returning to fill the landscape with song, and increased hours of sunlight. New life is awakening inside of us, too—we are part of nature's rhythms.

Write/draw/doodle your hopes and intentions for the week ahead. Consider what feels like it's "waking up" in your life. There may be new opportunities or experiences coming up—or you may be open to a new awareness or perspective about a circumstance in your life. At times, challenges in our lives awaken us to something we hadn't known or sensed before.

Some prompts to spark your reflections

I hope to awaken ...

What's awakening around me is/are ...

I am grateful for these awakenings because ...

Date: / /

Searching for signs and symbols

Notice where the theme of *awakening* shows up this week in your dreams, landscape, or imagination. Spend time outdoors and notice any signs of new life. Notice when your spirit feels activated and full of energy.

Write/draw/doodle about the awakening *connections that you find around you.*

Beauty awakens the soul to act.

Dante Alighieri

Embracing mindfulness

Make a list of everything that is beautiful around you. Think of nature, art, people, and beautiful experiences. Select one and describe it in detail. What does this beautiful thing awaken in your soul?

Weekly practice

Through the coming week, take your journal and spend some time in your neighborhood, writing about what you notice "waking up" around you. You may feel inspired about a particular thing and want to write more about it and how this part of nature reminds you of the power of awakening.

Weekly theme

Planting seeds

Setting intentions

Anyone who has tended a garden knows that spring is a time for planting seeds. Seeds need to be sown in soil, spaced out evenly, covered properly, and given the right amount of water. Planting seeds is a wonderful springtime metaphor for taking small steps to bring new things we desire to life!

Write/draw/doodle your hopes and intentions for the week ahead. Think about the steps you're taking to generate changes, growth, or new adventures into your life. They can be small steps, just like placing a seed into the ground.

Some prompts to spark your reflections

I'm laying the groundwork for ...

I'm excited to ...

Step by step, I can ...

Date: / /

Searching for signs and symbols

Notice where the theme of *planting seeds* shows up this week in your dreams, landscape, or imagination. If you don't normally spend time digging in the dirt, this could be a week to try planting some real seeds and see what metaphors come to mind.

Write/draw/doodle about the planting seeds *connections that you find around you.*

He who plants a tree
Plants a hope.

Lucy Larcom

Embracing mindfulness

Planting is an act of faith, hope, and trust. During difficult times, planting is even an act of resilience. Think about the kinds of seeds that you're planting—and affirm how courageous it is to take any step towards growth and change.

Weekly practice

A helpful way to nurture the metaphorical seeds that you're planting is through visualization. Find a comfortable position, take some deep breaths, and imagine what it would look and feel like for the steps you're taking to grow into fruition. As you breathe, affirm that your seeds are taking root.

Weekly theme

Dawn

Setting intentions

Just as dawn marks a fresh start after the darkness of night, spring brings renewal and new life after the long winter. In many traditions, dawn is a sacred time for meditation, prayer, or reflection—a moment to open the day with connection and grounding.

Write/draw/doodle your hopes and intentions for the week ahead. Consider how you might use the early hours of the day to set your intentions for the season. What in your life is ready for a fresh start? How can this season be a time of creation?

Some prompts to spark your reflections

In the dawn hours, I sense ...

After the darkness of winter, I'm ready to ...

I am grateful for these new beginnings ...

Date: / /

Searching for signs and symbols

Notice where the theme of *dawn* shows up this week in your dreams, landscape, or imagination. If you're not usually an early riser, try setting an alarm one morning to experience the quiet magic of dawn. Watch the sky lighten, listen for birdsong, or notice other signs of awakening around you. In Roman mythology, Aurora was the goddess of dawn who flew across the sky each morning to introduce the sun—you might want to envision her as you watch the sunrise.

Write/draw/doodle about the dawn *connections that you find around you.*

The breeze
at dawn
has secrets
to tell you.
Don’t go back
to sleep.

Rumi

Embracing mindfulness

Reflect on Rumi's words. Take a morning to sit quietly and listen to the breeze or other early sounds. Imagine these sounds are whispers of wisdom or secrets meant just for you. What messages do you hear?

Weekly practice

Throughout the week, make a list of the things in your life that are calling for dawning—a clean slate or a gentle rebirth. It could be a pattern you've outgrown, a space in your home that needs refreshing, or even a project you once set aside but now feel ready to return to. Choose one item from your list and give it some loving attention.

Weekly theme

Cleansing

Setting intentions

Spring cleaning is an ancient tradition around the world to get rid of dirt accumulated through the winter months. Cleansing, the process of cleaning something out, can apply to our inner worlds as well as outer worlds.

Write/draw/doodle your hopes and intentions for the week ahead. Think about how springtime energy, more sunlight, and warmer weather can motivate your cleansing.

Some prompts to spark your reflections

When I open the windows, I feel ...

It's satisfying to clean ...

I am ready for a new beginning ...

Date: / /

Searching for signs and symbols

Notice where the theme of *cleansing* shows up this week in your dreams, landscape, or imagination. Water is a symbol associated with cleansing. This could be a good week to visit a lake, stream, or other water source. If it's warm enough, dip in your toes for a symbolic cleansing ritual!

Write/draw/doodle about the cleansing *connections that you find around you.*

Throw open the windows of your soul to the sun.

Marcus Aurelius

Embracing mindfulness

Our emotional and spiritual lives are connected to our physical bodies and surroundings. Open windows, get rid of clutter, scrub your floors ... and pay attention to how spring cleaning affects your spirit and energy.

Weekly practice

During the winter months, our muscles and joints can become tight and strained. Try some gentle stretching in the mornings or evenings, take a daily walk outdoors, and seek out natural light whenever you can. Movement is another kind of cleansing, releasing the old and welcoming what's new!

Weekly theme

Sunshine

Setting intentions

From the spring equinox, sunshine increases each day. Sunshine—direct sunlight, unbroken by clouds—represents clarity, warmth, and life-giving energy. Sunshine is especially welcome after the dark, cold, and barren winter months.

Write/draw/doodle your hopes and intentions for the week ahead. Consider how spring sunshine affects your physical and emotional wellbeing—your sleep cycle, your mood, and your energy level.

Some prompts to spark your reflections
With greater sunshine, I can ...
What's being illuminated in my life is ...
This week, I'm grateful for ...

Date: / /

Searching for signs and symbols

Notice where the theme of *sunshine* shows up this week in your dreams, landscape, or imagination. The sun is revered across cultures, representing life and vitality. Symbols of the sun can be found in contemporary and historical art, jewelry, and pottery; in stories and fables.

Write/draw/doodle about the sunshine *connections that you find around you.*

Give me
the splendid
silent sun
with all his beams
full-dazzling ...

Walt Whitman

Embracing mindfulness

Nature is full of "silent" forces that we often take for granted. This week, pay attention to the sun's presence. Imagine a day without the sun rising. Express your gratitude to the sun in spoken or written words.

Weekly practice

If you practice yoga, you're probably familiar with the sun salutation. This series, traditionally performed at dawn, is a wonderful practice to warm up the body, honor the sun, and connect body, mind, and spirit. If yoga is new to you, find a video of the sun salutation and give it a try. Repeat for a few days outdoors in the fresh air and notice how doing a sun salutation (or two!) immersed in sunshine makes you feel.

Weekly theme

Honoring earth

Setting intentions

Nature reawakens in the spring and witnessing this process can reawaken our desire to honor the earth and deepen our connection to its cycles. Now more than ever, honoring the earth is an essential human value and we can begin by focusing on our personal connection to our planet.

Write/draw/doodle your hopes and intentions for the week ahead. Think about ways of honoring earth and be a mirror of springtime reawakening.

Some prompts to spark your reflections

I feel connected to nature when ...

I show my appreciation for the planet by ...

I am grateful to the earth for ...

Date: /   /

Searching for signs and symbols

Notice where the theme of *honoring earth* shows up this week in your dreams, landscape, or imagination. Budding trees and blossoming flowers represent life force and renewal. Eggs, butterflies, and rabbits are all spring symbols of earth's rebirth.

Write/draw/doodle about the honoring earth *connections that you find around you.*

Man's heart
away from nature
becomes hard.

Luther Standing Bear

Embracing mindfulness

Spring calls us to witness the earth awakening from winter. Take off your shoes and feel the earth beneath your feet. Plant seeds in soil. Sketch, take photos, or capture in words the beautiful or surprising things you see coming back to life.

Weekly practice

Make a commitment to take care of the earth with small, manageable actions. You might get involved with local community efforts like supporting a community garden or recycling initiative. None of us can create systemic change on our own, but by working together, we can have a significant impact.

Weekly theme

Festivity

Setting intentions

Across cultures, spring is a time for celebrations. From pagan holidays including Ostara (celebrating the equinox) and Beltane (May Day) to Easter in the Christian tradition and Passover in the Jewish tradition, these festivities all share themes related to rebirth, freedom, and renewal in different ways.

Write/draw/doodle your hopes and intentions for the week ahead. Think about an upcoming festivity that you're looking forward to and your favorite parts of preparing for and experiencing them.

Some prompts to spark your reflections

I love to celebrate ...
I feel joyful when ...
I can enhance festivities by ...

Date: / /

Searching for signs and symbols

Notice where the theme of *festivity* shows up this week in your dreams, landscape, or imagination. You might research holiday symbols from your own culture or faith tradition, or enjoy reading about festive spring symbols from other cultures.

Write/draw/doodle about the festivity *connections that you find around you.*

Life is a festival only to the wise.

Ralph Waldo Emerson

Embracing mindfulness

Festive days come periodically, but daily life can be full of joy and celebration when we live with gratitude for our lives. Imagine each day this week as a time to celebrate and notice how that shifts your experience of the day.

Weekly practice

In Japan, Shunbun no Hi is a national holiday that celebrates the spring equinox. Festivities include going with family and friends to view the blooming cherry blossom trees. Create your own flower-viewing festivity this week, whether you invite a friend for a spring picnic, visit a beautiful garden, or take a nature walk to look for wildflowers.

Weekly theme

Energy

Setting intentions

Springtime offers us the chance to renew our energy—the strength and vitality needed for life. It's time for forward momentum, dusting off the sleepiness of winter, and planting new seeds.

Write/draw/doodle your hopes and intentions for the week ahead. Pay attention to your physical and emotional energy. Spring can be a time for mirroring nature and opening our emotional lives, just as the flowers open.

Some prompts to spark your reflections

I feel energized when ...
With renewed energy, I can ...
More and more, I notice that ...

Date: / /

Searching for signs and symbols

Notice where the theme of *energy* shows up this week in your dreams, landscape, or imagination. Many cultures have symbols like a hamsa, pentacle, or other talisman created to protect your energy from negative forces.

Write/draw/doodle about the energy *connections that you find around you.*

I believe a leaf of grass is no less than the journey-work of the stars ...

Walt Whitman

Embracing mindfulness

It's easy to forget that even something as small as a blade of grass is alive and full of its own life force. Turn off all of your devices and take a walk, paying attention to the natural world. Notice how your energy shifts.

Weekly practice

Springtime is full of new sights and sounds—and also smells. Aromas can stimulate our limbic system, arousing and boosting energy. Take a walk outdoors, concentrating on your sense of smell. Notice how your energy shifts when you encounter scents like lilac, honeysuckle, or jasmine. Breathing deeply to inhale the smell of spring also awakens energy!

Weekly theme

Connection

Setting intentions

Connection occurs when we're linked to another person, thing, idea, element, or part of nature. During the winter months, we may feel more inner-focused and less outwardly connected. Spring energy calls us out of our homes to reconnect with friends and community as well as with the natural world.

Write/draw/doodle your hopes and intentions for the week ahead. Think about the connections in your life that are strong and vital, and also those that might need some tending. This could be a great week to take steps to reconnect with someone or something important to you.

Some prompts to spark your reflections

I value my connections with ...

I hope to reconnect with ...

I feel connected to nature when ...

Date: / /

Searching for signs and symbols

Notice where the theme of *connection* shows up this week in your dreams, landscape, or imagination. There are many ancient symbols representing how life is interconnected: the infinity symbol, the tree of life, and the lotus flower are a few examples. You may have your own symbols for connections, like a ring, a tattoo, or another item that binds you to a special person in your life.

Write/draw/doodle about the connection *signs and symbols that you find around you.*

The slightest movement matters to all of nature; the entire sea changes for a single stone.

Blaise Pascal

Embracing mindfulness

Make a list of people who have influenced your life in a positive way—teachers, friends, colleagues, neighbors, or anyone who has encouraged or inspired you. Choose one of them and write them a letter, expressing your gratitude. If the person is alive, send them your letter!

Weekly practice

Pay attention to when and where you feel a sense of connection—and when you feel disconnected. What's happening in the settings or activities when you feel connected? What might shift or change during the times or places when connections don't feel as strong?

Weekly theme

Beauty

Setting intentions

Beauty is defined as a combination of qualities, including shape, color, and form, that please our aesthetic senses. During spring, the mix of vibrant colors, fragrant blooms, and returning birdsong arouses our senses. When spring's canvas arrives, we can experience the beauty all around us, as if the earth itself is a work of art.

Write/draw/doodle your hopes and intentions for the week ahead. Consider how the beautiful things in the natural world inspire and delight you and how expansively you understand the idea of beauty.

Some prompts to spark your reflections

I take time to notice ...

More and more, I value these beautiful things ...

I am thankful for the beauty of ...

Date: / /

Searching for signs and symbols

Notice where the theme of *beauty* shows up this week in your dreams, landscape, or imagination. Mythology brings us goddesses from across cultures: the Greek Aphrodite, the Roman Venus, the Norse Freya, and the Egyptian Hathor, who represent beauty, love, and desire.

Write/draw/doodle about the beauty *connections that you find around you.*

Everything has beauty, but not everyone sees it.

Confucius

Embracing mindfulness

The ability to recognize beauty depends on our awareness and our perception. Every culture has its own "beauty standards" but we don't need to be limited by those often narrow parameters. We can discover beautiful things through our own senses and inner knowing.

Weekly practice

Beauty as a concept can feel complicated and even painful because of the commercialization and exploitation within the "beauty industry." Techniques like mirror work can help to work through internalized criticism. Take time out to look in a mirror at your reflection. Offer a positive affirmation, which could be as simple as "I love you." Take some deep breaths and repeat the affirmation several times. Notice how this practice makes you feel. Remember, there is not one kind of flower in the natural world, but many—with different colors, sizes, shapes, and smells. Each human is beautiful in their own way.

Weekly theme

Embodiment

Setting intentions

Embodiment refers to our experience of living within our physical bodies. After the long winter, spring is a time to reawaken our bodies through outdoor activities and time in nature. We also recognize aspects of nature, like blossoming trees, that serve as the embodiment of spring.

Write/draw/doodle your hopes and intentions for the week ahead. Think about ways that you can connect to the season through physical, emotional, and mindfulness practices that help you reconnect with body, mind, and spirit.

Some prompts to spark your reflections

I feel my body calm when ...

More and more, I am grounded in my body because ...

I am thankful to experience ...

Date: / /

Searching for signs and symbols

Notice where the theme of *embodiment* shows up this week in your dreams, landscape, or imagination. Immersing yourself in nature can open you to all kinds of living things that represent the embodiment of spring. Think of butterflies, ladybugs, birds, and sunrises, along with all kinds of flowers and flowering trees.

Write/draw/doodle about the embodiment *connections that you find around you.*

Every atom belonging to me as good belongs to you.

Walt Whitman

Embracing mindfulness

Our physical bodies can remind us of interconnection—with ourselves, with other humans, and with all living things. We're each given a body to care for and attend. It's easy to take that gift for granted. This week, gently offer your body some extra tender loving care.

Weekly practice

A body scan is a simple mindfulness practice that helps us to observe sensations in our bodies and release tension. You can do a simple body scan anywhere, but sitting outdoors in the spring air and scanning your body can be a powerful experience. Close your eyes and take a few moments to breathe deeply and scan through your body, moving from your toes, relaxing each part of your body, up through to your head. Notice how the fresh air on your face and the sunlight around you affect how parts of your body feel.

Weekly theme

Joy

Setting intentions

Joy—the feeling of great happiness or pleasure—can be felt all year long, but the spectacle of new life that takes place during the spring creates an atmosphere that especially invokes joy. Different from fleeting happiness, joy is being filled with gratitude and the acknowledgement that life is full of good as well as challenging things.

Write/draw/doodle your hopes and intentions for the week ahead. Think about what the experience of joy means to you and how you stay open to joy, even alongside feelings of sadness.

Some prompts to spark your reflections

I find great pleasure in ...

Joyful feelings bubble up when ...

The experience of spring ...

Date: / /

Searching for signs and symbols

Notice where the theme of *joy* shows up this week in your dreams, landscape, or imagination. In many cultures, bluebirds and hummingbirds are symbols of happiness. You may find a Laughing Buddha where you least expect it! There may be people or animal companions in your life who symbolize a joyful feeling.

Write/draw/doodle about the joy *connections that you find around you.*

A light exists in spring
Not present on the year
At any other period.

Emily Dickinson

Embracing mindfulness

The beauty and energy of spring can be a natural joy elixir! Very often, we hold back from experiencing joy because we know that there is so much suffering and pain in the world. But noticing joy doesn't mean turning away from hard things. Let the light in spring guide you towards experiencing joyful moments.

Weekly practice

We can spread a feeling of joy to others in simple and easy ways. Think about how you might surprise a friend or loved one with a little treat, a love note, or a bouquet of wildflowers. Invite a coworker to go outside and take a walk with you during lunchtime. Share native plants or seeds with a neighbor. Offer a genuine smile to people you pass.

Spring reflections

When we pay attention to seasonal transitions, they can become powerful gateways to new adventures and opportunities. Take a moment to reflect on the awakenings, connections, joy, and festivities that you have experienced this spring. You may also want to acknowledge any challenges or grief that shaped these past months. Write down the insights and wisdom you've gathered—gifts that can enrich your life as you step into summer.

Make this reflection page as interactive and personal as you like! You might paste in a ticket stub from a favorite film, play, or concert; a memento from a spring celebration; a photo or two; even a pressed flower, feather, or twig you collected on a nature outing.

Some prompts to spark your reflections

Favorite people I shared time with ...

Beautiful places I experienced ...

New and enjoyable activities ...

Times when I felt vibrant, connected, alive ...

All that I hope to release ...

Wisdom I'm carrying into the new season ...

Presence
Ritual
Animation
S U M
Radiance
Growth
Creativity

Savoring

Rest

M E R

Cycles

Haven

Serenade

Fire

During summer, the natural world bursts with light, heat, and life. It's a season of growth, creativity, and abundance—both in nature and within ourselves.

We're invited to savor summer's fullness: the long golden days, the hum of insects, the pulse of warm air, and even the sudden relief of summer storms. These moments remind us of nature's vibrant rhythm and our own inner fire. Summer can feel like a haven, when the whole world hums with vitality and song.

These prompts are designed to help you move through summer attuned to your own radiance and creative energy. You can return to them anytime, in any season—whenever you feel fiery and alive, noticing your growth and presence.

Weekly theme

Ritual

Setting intentions

A ritual is a kind of ceremony, full of intention and meaning, meant to connect us to our inner spirit. We all have daily rituals that are important to us—like making our morning cup of coffee or kissing a loved one before bed. Ancient civilizations came together at the start of summer for special rituals and celebrations to honor the longest day of the year. You may want to create your own summer solstice ritual to welcome the new season!

Write/draw/doodle your hopes and intentions for the week ahead. Consider what kind of ritual would best help you to transition from spring to summer. What are your wishes for the months ahead?

Some prompts to spark your reflections

I welcome summer by ...

May summer be full of ...

I'm grateful that summer is here because ...

Date: / /

Searching for signs and symbols

Notice where the theme of *ritual* shows up this week in your dreams, landscape, or imagination. Consider Stonehenge, which was likely built around 2500 BCE to align with the summer solstice sunrise. You might create a summer altar full of meaningful items such as flowers and herbs, candles, and solar symbols.

Write/draw/doodle about the ritual *connections that you find around you.*

Shall I compare thee to
a summer's day?
Thou art more lovely
and more temperate ...

William Shakespeare

Embracing mindfulness

The longer days of summer can activate our social nature. Think of someone you hope to connect with over the season. Write them an inviting note or letter with your hopes to create a special summer outing together!

Weekly practice

Through the coming week, pay attention to what kinds of rituals permeate your day that you may not give much thought to. Add some summer sparkle to them! For example, a simple morning coffee can become extra special when you take it outdoors. Dinner can be packed up as a picnic and taken to a park. Yoga or stretching can be done outdoors while you watch the sun setting.

Weekly theme

Presence

Setting intentions

Presence is about what's happening right now, in this very moment. In the lushness of summer, we feel the sun's warmth during long days, witness flowers blooming and fruits ripening, experience summer storms, and notice the lively rhythms of birds and animals. Summer invites us to set aside distractions and awaken our senses to the quiet magic unfolding all around us.

Write/draw/doodle your hopes and intentions for the week ahead. Consider what helps you stay present to both your inner and outer worlds. When you are truly present, what new possibilities begin to unfold?

Some prompts to spark your reflections

When I notice that I'm distracted, I can ...

I feel most present when ...

I want to be present for/because ...

Date: / /

Searching for signs and symbols

Notice where the theme of *presence* shows up this week in your dreams, landscape, or imagination. Spend time outdoors to experience the presence of a sunrise or sunset. If you're able to gaze at the moon or the stars from where you live, notice how you feel in their presence.

Write/draw/doodle about the presence *connections that you find around you.*

To live is so startling, it leaves but little room for other occupations ...

Emily Dickinson

Embracing mindfulness

Think of something you saw, heard, or felt today that startled you with its presence. Have you sometimes taken that thing for granted? Describe what helps you to be present to what's happening inside and around you.

Weekly practice

Through the coming week, try to pay attention to when your mind is drifting into busy thoughts or worries. Take a few long, deep breaths to return to your body. Look at (or listen to) what's happening right now around you. Offer gratitude for one (or more!) thing(s) in your presence.

Weekly theme

Radiance

Setting intentions

To radiate means to emit energy or rays. That's the work of the amazing sun—and we can also recognize how each of us sends out our unique energy.

Write/draw/doodle your hopes and intentions for the week ahead. Consider what gives you energy—both inside and around you. What are some ways that you can spread and share your energy with the world around you?

Some prompts to spark your reflections

I share my energy when ...

I feel energized by ...

Others experience my radiance when ...

Date: / /

Searching for signs and symbols

Notice where the theme of *radiance* shows up this week in your dreams, landscape, or imagination. Radiance might come through a song lyric or a memory from summer days gone by. It's that sudden zap of energy, like sunlight bursting through clouds.

Write/draw/doodle about the radiance *connections that you find around you.*

There are two ways of spreading light: to be The candle or the mirror that reflects it.

Edith Wharton

Embracing mindfulness

Remember a moment when you shared rays of love, compassion, and openheartedness with someone. Remember a moment when you received that kind of light. Describe how that feels.

Weekly practice

Through the coming week, notice when you experience moments of radiant energy when you're outdoors. The feeling might come from noticing the warmth of the sun on your face or the joy of being surrounded by vibrant flowers and blossoming trees. What relationships/experiences/landscapes fill you with energy and light?

Weekly theme

Animation

Setting intentions

The word animate comes from the Latin for "bestowing of life." Summer is when the seeds planted in spring come to fruition. It's a time to notice what is stirring within us—what brings our lives purpose and richness.

Write/draw/doodle your hopes and intentions for the week ahead. Consider what is coming to life within you—and what you hope to animate even more.

Some prompts to spark your reflections

More and more, I sense a strong life force when ...

Things that make me feel alive include ...

I'm grateful for all that is coming to life ...

Date: / /

Searching for signs and symbols

Notice where the theme of *animation* shows up this week in your dreams, landscape, or imagination. During summer, your sense of desire may be more animated. The season invites sensory and sensual exploration: the abundance of ripe fruits to taste, the feeling of water against your skin, the quiet that comes after a thunderstorm.

Write/draw/doodle about the animation *connections that you find around you.*

The morning-glory
blooms but
for an hour,
Yet it differs not
at heart from
the giant pine.

From *Zenrin-kushū*

Embracing mindfulness

Think about a part of the natural world you've seen recently that is full of life—it may be a house plant, something growing in a garden, a wild mushroom, or something subtle and quiet like a stirring wind. Describe what you notice about its vigor and energy, and how it's similar or different from your own life force.

Weekly practice

Throughout the week, bring a spirit of playful curiosity to whatever might animate you. Wander through a different neighborhood, taste a summer fruit you've never tried, or listen to music that's new to you. Stay open to what might enliven your spirit in fresh—and pleasurable—ways.

Weekly theme

Growth

Setting intentions

Growth often means increasing in physical size, but we can also think of it as expanding our emotional and spiritual capacity. In climates with changing seasons, summer is a season of abundance. Fields, gardens, and wild spaces brim with color and life. What was once just a seed in spring now stands tall, ripe, and ready.

Write/draw/doodle your hopes and intentions for the week ahead. Reflect on the ways you have grown, ways you are growing, and ways you long to grow during this summer season.

Some prompts to spark your reflections

More and more, I sense myself growing when ...

I am inspired by the growth I see in ...

I hope to grow ...

Date: / /

Searching for signs and symbols

Notice where the theme of *growth* shows up this week in your dreams, landscape, or imagination. Spend time with growing things: wildflowers, vegetable gardens, trees, and vines.

Write/draw/doodle about the growth *connections that you find around you.*

All things are up
and growing;
only the spirit
that slumbers not
in man keeps pace
with them.

Frederick William Faber

Embracing mindfulness

We are always growing, though sometimes we can't sense our own growth. Look back over photos from summer a year ago, or even a decade ago, or going back to your childhood. Describe what comes up for you about how your wisdom and understanding have deepened or changed since that time.

Weekly practice

Calm and quiet is essential for growth. Sometimes we are so busy "doing" that we neglect rest time. Allow yourself time to slow down, get extra sleep, or take time for the kinds of rituals that help you to relax.

Weekly theme

Creativity

Setting intentions

Creativity springs from our imagination—it's the spark that lets us dream, experiment, and bring fresh ideas into being. In the longer, sunlit days of summer, we're invited to play, explore, and try new things—simple acts that nourish our creative spirit.

Write/draw/doodle your hopes and intentions for the week ahead. Consider what helps your personal creativity flow and what small steps you might take to welcome more creative energy into your days this week.

Some prompts to spark your reflections

I feel most alive with creative ideas when ...
I am creating a life filled with ...
Connecting with my creativity feels ...

Date: / /

Searching for signs and symbols

Notice where the theme of *creativity* shows up this week in your dreams, landscape, or imagination. Surround yourself with artists who inspire you: listen to songs you love, revisit favorite poems, or linger with visual art that moves you.

Write/draw/doodle about the creativity *connections that you find around you.*

Every child is an artist. The problem is how to remain an artist once we grow up.

Pablo Picasso

Embracing mindfulness

Summer is the perfect season to revisit the activities that once made you feel happy and free as a child. Maybe you stayed up late to catch fireflies, splashed in a creek or lake, or built sandcastles under the sun. Our inner child longs for that sense of freedom and play. When we allow them space, we awaken joy—and breathe fresh life into our creative spirit.

Weekly practice

Try a creative activity that's completely new to you, approaching it with a spirit of curiosity. Take a dance class, experiment with a new recipe, or gather leaves, shells, or stones to make a nature-inspired collage. Pay attention to how you feel as you awaken creative muscles that have been resting, and notice the fresh energy that emerges.

Weekly theme

Savoring

Setting intentions

Savoring means tasting something and enjoying it completely. We can savor food and wine, but we can also bring that quality of attention and enjoyment to our activities, conversations, and surroundings. Summer is full of fresh tastes to savor.

Write/draw/doodle your hopes and intentions for the week ahead. Consider what kinds of experiences you savor—and what you might invite into your life this week to completely enjoy. No experience or taste is too big or small to savor.

Some prompts to spark your reflections

I want to savor ...

I find total enjoyment when ...

I give myself permission to savor ...

Date: / /

Searching for signs and symbols

Notice where the theme of *savoring* shows up this week in your dreams, landscape, or imagination. Maybe you visit a new farmers' market, try a recipe you've been longing to make, or find a body of water in which to cool off from the intensity of summer heat.

Write/draw/doodle about the savoring *connections that you find around you.*

The purpose of life is to live it, to taste experience to the utmost.

Eleanor Roosevelt

Embracing mindfulness

It's natural for humans to ruminate on what's behind us and to worry about what's ahead. Savoring experiences can help us be more present in the here and now. Describe one sensory experience (a delicious cold drink that refreshed you from the heat, a moment with your animal companion, the feel of summer rain on your skin) that you were able to savor today or sometime this week.

Weekly practice

Give yourself permission to enjoy something completely every day. You may need to turn off your phone, head outdoors, and take some deep breaths. Then try eating a piece of fruit or sipping a cold iced tea. Notice how you feel when you savor with intention.

Weekly theme

Rest

Setting intentions

Rest is a state of full relaxation, allowing us to refresh and gather our strength. Human beings need sleep, but there are other restful activities that we can integrate throughout our day to recharge our spirits. The languid heat of summer months invites us to take a power nap in a hammock, step outside for a midday breath of fresh air, or sip on a cold, calming tea.

Write/draw/doodle your hopes and intentions for the week ahead. Consider how you could take short breaks for rest during busy days, and what kinds of experiences feel most restful for you.

Some prompts to spark your reflections

I am able to rest when ...

When I take time to relax, I notice ...

Rest is essential because ...

Date: / /

Searching for signs and symbols
Notice where the theme of *rest* shows up this week in your dreams, landscape, or imagination. In Greek mythology, the goddess Pasithea represents rest and relaxation. Can you think of characters in pop culture or literature who embody the kind of rest you're seeking?

Write/draw/doodle about the rest *connections that you find around you.*

Rest is not idleness,
and to lie sometimes
on the grass ...
is by no means
a waste of time.

John Lubbock

Embracing mindfulness

We live in a culture that does not encourage us to rest, yet rest is vital for physical, emotional, and creative health. If you feel resistance coming up when you think about resting, consider where it's coming from. What messages have you received about taking rest time? How might you shift those messages?

Weekly practice

This week, allow yourself more down time than usual. You might nap, daydream, lie in the grass, or do something else that feels restful to you. Notice how your energy changes when you take some time to rest.

Weekly theme

Cycles

Setting intentions

Cycles are patterns of events that take place in a particular order. Nature's seasons are a kind of cycle. We move through winter, spring, summer, and autumn throughout our lives. Each time we enter a season, we can experience it as new.

Write/draw/doodle your hopes and intentions for the week ahead. Consider how this summer has been the same or different from other summers in your life. Think back to childhood and teenage years, and how summer felt then as compared to what your adult summers have been like.

Some prompts to spark your reflections

This summer feels different because ...

I notice that this summer ...

I remember how summer used to feel ...

Date: / /

Searching for signs and symbols

Notice where the theme of *cycles* shows up this week in your dreams, landscape, or imagination. What do you encounter that takes you back and forth in time? What kinds of traditions were part of your summers gone by? What songs, sights, or tastes help you return to them again?

Write/draw/doodle about the cycles *connections that you find around you.*

Look into nature,
and then you will
understand it better.

Albert Einstein

Embracing mindfulness

Ancient agricultural civilizations lived in rhythm with nature's cycles. Wisdom grew from this connection and mystical traditions sprang from noticing how the cycles of the seasons mirror the cycles of human life. How has looking into nature helped your understanding of life?

Weekly practice

Every day has its own kind of cycle. This week, notice how your energy and imagination shift through the early morning to noontime to mid-afternoon to dusk and into the evening. When are you most receptive to your creativity?

Weekly theme

Haven

Setting intentions

A haven is a place of refuge or safety, a sanctuary offering comfort in peace. Each season offers us different kinds of havens, right in our surroundings. Anywhere that you find peace and tranquility can be a haven. Think of an air-conditioned movie theater, a favorite outdoor café, or a beautiful lake ... anywhere that provides a sense of peace in the summer months.

Write/draw/doodle your hopes and intentions for the week ahead. Consider places where you find a sense of peace during challenges that come up in your life.

Some prompts to spark your reflections

I feel at peace when ...

More and more, I find tranquility in ...

My secret summer havens are ...

Date: / /

Searching for signs and symbols

Notice where the theme of *haven* shows up this week in your dreams, landscape, or imagination. A haven could be a physical retreat or an emotional space. Look for quiet retreats in your day, spaces where you feel relaxed and at ease. What visual cues signal that you're entering a haven?

Write/draw/doodle about the haven *connections that you find around you.*

Come to the woods, for here is rest. There is no repose like that of the green deep woods ...

John Muir

Embracing mindfulness

Wherever you are, certain activities can initiate a sense of peace. John Muir wrote about finding a moment to rest in the deep green woods. Deep breathing can also give us a sense of calm, as can closing our eyes for a minute or two. How can you create a haven from wherever you happen to be?

Weekly practice

This week is an ideal time to seek out a new haven right in your surroundings. Invite in a sense of curiosity and exploration, and using the qualities of "haven" you've journaled about, go and search for a peaceful place that's out there, waiting for you.

Weekly theme

Serenade

Setting intentions

A serenade is a piece of music, generally sung in the open air. The landscape of summer can feel like a long serenade, with all varieties of birds and also cicadas, grasshoppers, and frogs adding their music as a soundscape. Longer evenings make space for outdoor concerts and the music of conversation when friends and neighbors gather.

Write/draw/doodle your hopes and intentions for the week ahead. Imagine that the summer season is singing its serenade just for you.

Some prompts to spark your reflections

I hear expressions of love when …

The summer sings to me by …

Joyful music makes me feel …

Date: / /

Searching for signs and symbols

Notice where the theme of *serenade* shows up this week in your dreams, landscape, or imagination. If you hear a particular kind of bird, for example, look up associations with its species. Check out summer music playlists that evoke different kinds of feelings for you—from nostalgia to playfulness or even melancholy.

Write/draw/doodle about the serenade *connections that you find around you.*

Where words fail,
music speaks.

Hans Christian Andersen

Embracing mindfulness

Sometimes music or song can connect us to feelings that we struggle to put into words. Notice when you feel yourself swept up in the feeling of beauty, joy, and harmony this week.

Weekly practice

How often do you sing out loud? Did you know that there are now studies that show the physiological benefits of singing? This week is a great time to try that practice, however it feels comfortable for you. Sing in the shower or the car. Serenade your animal companions, your plants, or a special someone to whom you'd like to offer your song.

Weekly theme

Fire

Setting intentions

Fire is a chemical combustion, but we can also feel the energy of fire in our bodies and spirits. The summer begins with solstice, when humans used to gather around a great bonfire. It closes shortly after the beautiful orange corn moon, which illuminated the evening so farmers could gather late summer crops. As summer transitions to autumn, we welcome the power of fire to accompany us into a darker season.

Write/draw/doodle your hopes and intentions for the week ahead. Consider when and where you feel the energy of fire in your life.

Some prompts to spark your reflections

I am passionate about ...

The fire inside me is ...

I want to burn away and release ...

Date: / /

Searching for signs and symbols

Notice where the theme of *fire* shows up this week in your dreams, landscape, or imagination. Different world cultures attribute various meanings to fire. One of the most powerful is the symbol of the phoenix rising from the ashes—rebirth following destruction. During summer, wildfires are part of a natural process for rebirth and the health of some forests and grasslands.

Write/draw/doodle about the fire *connections that you find around you.*

The blazing fire makes flame and brightness out of everything that is thrown into it.

Marcus Aurelius

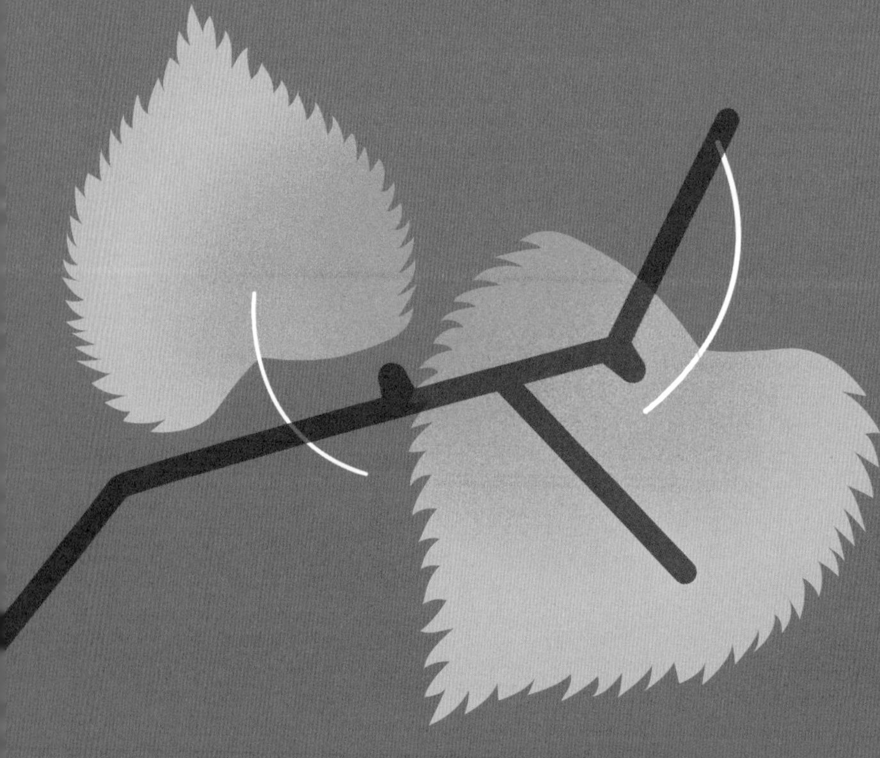

Embracing mindfulness

We can imagine an inner fire as a flame that ignites our spirit. All fires need tending. How do you nurture your spirit? What ignites your passions? Notice how different your inner fire feels when it's fed.

Weekly practice

Because fire can symbolize transformation, it's a powerful tool to help us release things that we no longer wish to carry. Writing a list of those things and burning it with a match or in a small fire can be a powerful practice, especially as you prepare to transition from summer to autumn.

Summer reflections

When we pay attention to seasonal transitions, they can become powerful gateways to new adventures and opportunities. Take a moment to reflect on the rest, growth, creativity, and radiance that you experienced this summer. You may also want to acknowledge the challenges or grief that shaped these past months. Write down the insights and wisdom you've gathered—gifts that can enrich your life as you step into autumn.

Make this reflection page as interactive and personal as you like! You might paste in a ticket stub from a favorite film, play, or concert; a souvenir from a vacation; a note from someone special; a photo or two; even a pressed flower or herb.

Some prompts to spark your reflections
Favorite people I shared time with ...
Beautiful places I experienced ...
New and enjoyable activities ...
Times when I felt vibrant, connected, alive ...
All that I hope to release ...
Wisdom I'm carrying into the new season ...

Beginnings

A U T

Balance

Majesty

Harvest

Celebration

Ancestors

Impermanence

Autumn is the season of majesty and transformation. The natural world blazes with vibrant color before gracefully letting go, returning its brilliance to the earth.

It's a time of harvest and gratitude, of gathering what we've grown, and celebrating the abundance of the year. As the nights grow longer, we're invited to honor our ancestors, embrace change, and reflect on the impermanence that shapes all life.

These prompts are designed to help you move through autumn as a season of balance and becoming—a time of transition, release, and renewal. You can return to them anytime, in any season—whenever you feel called to let go and begin again.

Gratitude

Letting go

U M N

Transition

Dusk

Transformation

Weekly theme

Beginnings

Setting intentions

At first, it may feel surprising to think of autumn as a season of beginnings. After all, it's the time of harvest, of leaves falling, of transition. Yet when we look closely, autumn is full of newness: harvesting makes space for transformation, and transformation opens the way for fresh starts.

Write/draw/doodle your hopes and intentions for the week ahead. Notice what's beginning to stir around you—whether it's external, like the energy of a new school term, or something more internal, like a new layer of self-discovery.

Some prompts to spark your reflections

This autumn, I welcome ...

What's waking up inside me now ...

I'm ready to start fresh with ...

Date: / /

Searching for signs and symbols

Notice where the theme of *beginnings* shows up this week in your dreams, landscape, or imagination. Across cultures, stories of beginnings—of the world, of life, of creativity—help us make sense of our own starts. Every creative act begins with a blank page, an empty canvas, a first step.

Write/draw/doodle about the beginnings *connections that you find around you.*

Spring is the morning of the year,
And summer is the noontide bright;
The autumn is the evening clear
That comes before the winter's night.

Frank Dempster Sherman

Embracing mindfulness

In some traditions, evening itself is the true beginning of a new day. In Dempster Sherman's words, autumn becomes part of the cycle: the luminous evening before winter's rest. In our own lives, too, we move through cycles of light and shadow, endings and beginnings—each one giving rise to the next.

Weekly practice

It takes courage to begin something new, whether it's a big event like a move to a new place or the start of a new job, or something smaller, like joining a club, trying a new hobby, or learning a new language. At the start, it's natural to feel tender, uncertain, or even alone. Remember: beginnings don't have to happen in isolation. Reach out to a friend or loved one. Share your process. Use this journal as a place to hold your feelings and to remind yourself: you don't have to begin alone.

Weekly theme

Balance

Setting intentions

At the autumn equinox, day and night stand in near-perfect balance. This moment in nature invites us to reflect on balance in our own lives—between activity and rest, solitude and connection, giving and receiving.

Write/draw/doodle your hopes and intentions for the week ahead. Notice where balance already feels steady, and where you might need to shift something small to restore a greater sense of harmony.

Some prompts to spark your reflections

I notice a sense of balance when ...

I'm seeking balance in ...

Standing in the way of balance in my life is ...

Date: / /

Searching for signs and symbols

Notice where the theme of *balance* shows up this week in your dreams, landscape, or imagination. The season of harmony, fairness, and alignment begins now. Autumn also offers its own images of balance, such as wreaths, circling the cycles of the seasons, and candles, offering inner light as nights grow longer.

Write/draw/doodle about the balance *connections that you find around you.*

Autumn is the mellower season, and what we lose in flowers we more than gain in fruits.

Samuel Butler

Embracing mindfulness

With summer blossoms fading, autumn ripens into abundance. Harvest season reminds us that balance includes both effort and reward, work and rest. In our own lives, this is a time to pause and appreciate the fruits of what we've tended and grown.

Weekly practice

Balance isn't only a metaphor—it's a daily practice. Our emotional, spiritual, and physical selves need ongoing care to stay aligned. Journaling can help us notice the patterns that tip us off balance and gently guide us back towards steadiness. Try committing to write in your journal each morning or evening. Note moments when you felt focused and grounded, as well as times when you felt scattered or depleted. After a few days, look back and see if any patterns of energy or emotion begin to emerge.

Weekly theme

Majesty

Setting intentions

Majesty refers to an especially impressive kind of beauty or dignity. Autumn's vibrant colors, crisp air, and golden sunsets hold a special kind of majesty that has captivated artists and poets through the centuries.

Write/draw/doodle your hopes and intentions for the week ahead. Consider how the majesty of the natural world can support and inspire you. Enter the week as an artist—appreciating the beauty around and inside of you.

Some prompts to spark your reflections

I am inspired by ...
The majesty of autumn helps me feel ...
It's time to appreciate ...

Date: / /

Searching for signs and symbols

Notice where the theme of *majesty* shows up this week in your dreams, landscape, or imagination. If you don't live in a place with autumn foliage, look at photos or artwork that capture autumn's beauty. What do autumn's colors represent for you?

Write/draw/doodle about the majesty *connections that you find around you.*

I cannot endure
to waste anything
so precious as
autumnal sunshine
by staying
in the house.

Nathaniel Hawthorne

Embracing mindfulness

Knowing that leaves will fall and the barrenness of winter will follow autumn's sun, you may feel especially called to spend time outdoors. Describe your favorite autumn outdoor activities, whether you draw from childhood memories or your present experience of the season.

Weekly practice

Experience autumn with all of your senses, not only your eyes. Find a place to sit and listen to leaves, wind, or water. Take a walk and feel your feet crunch leaves; pick up pine cones and hold them in your hands. Notice how this full sensory experience enhances your gratitude for autumn—and for life itself.

Weekly theme

Harvest

Setting intentions

Just as autumn is a time of harvesting crops, it can also be an ideal time for us to reflect on what we've nurtured in our own lives. Think of autumn as a time for an "inner harvest."

Write/draw/doodle your hopes and intentions for the week ahead. Consider what you've given energy and attention to over the past year that is now flourishing.

Some prompts to spark your reflections
My life is full with ...
I feel my efforts paying off when ...
I have an abundance of ...

Date: / /

Searching for signs and symbols

Notice where the theme of *harvest* shows up this week in your dreams, landscape, or imagination. One very special autumn symbol is the harvest moon, the full moon closest to the autumn equinox. The harvest moon marks the end of the growing season, a time of abundance on the earth.

Write/draw/doodle about the harvest *connections that you find around you.*

The thankful receiver bears a plentiful harvest.

William Blake

Embracing mindfulness

Harvest is deeply tied to gratitude—an appreciation for food, friends, and the many gifts of life. Gratitude can become a conscious practice when we take time to name at least one thing—big or small—that strengthens or sustains us every day.

Weekly practice

Unlike a physical harvest, it can be harder to recognize the fruits of our inner lives. Throughout the week, pay attention to the ways you've grown emotionally and spiritually. What qualities have you cultivated since last autumn? Which ones were hard-won, and which now feel abundant within you?

Weekly theme

Celebration

Setting intentions

Cultures around the world have special celebrations that take place during autumn (in the northern hemisphere)—from Halloween and Dia De Muertos to Oktoberfest and Diwali, Sukkot in the Jewish tradition, the feast of St Clement in Italy, and the Harvest Moon Festival in China and so many more harvest festivals. Each of these celebrations includes special gatherings, ceremonies, foods, and rituals.

Write/draw/doodle your hopes and intentions for the week ahead. Consider how upcoming autumn celebrations can enhance your appreciation for the season.

Some prompts to spark your reflections

When I celebrate ...

I am looking forward to ...

I feel the magic of autumn when ...

Date: / /

Searching for signs and symbols

Notice where the theme of *celebration* shows up this week in your dreams, landscape, or imagination. Our cultural traditions are full of resonant symbols, each with different feelings. Some people love Halloween for its spookiness, while others are drawn to the play and mischief in dressing up.

Write/draw/doodle about the celebration *connections that you find around you.*

It's the first day
of autumn!
A time of hot
chocolatey mornings,
and toasty
marshmallow
evenings, and,
best of all, leaping
into leaves!

Winnie the Pooh

Embracing mindfulness

Winnie the Pooh expresses the celebratory joy, excitement, and energy that many of us felt in the autumn of our childhoods. Through our lives, we can find new and enjoyable ways to celebrate the season on our own, with friends and family, or simply by savoring the season.

Weekly practice

Autumn is a great time to either explore a new way to celebrate a familiar holiday or check out a cultural celebration that's unfamiliar to you. Be open to learning about different kinds of traditions and practices, foods, and customs. Celebrations of all kinds can enhance the richness of our lives.

Weekly theme

Ancestors

Setting intentions

Our ancestors include all of the people we are descended from—but we also can think of emotional or spiritual ancestors as being those individuals who have guided or inspired our lives. Because the autumn season mirrors cycles of life and death, loss and rebirth, it is associated with ancestors in many cultures. Spend some time outdoors this week among trees shedding their leaves, noticing the earthy scent of decay that nourishes new life. Feel how the turning world holds the memory of all that has lived before.

Write/draw/doodle your hopes and intentions for the week ahead. Consider all of the ways you have been, and continue to be, guided by the wisdom of your familial or spiritual ancestors—and how nature itself can be one of your teachers.

Some prompts to spark your reflections

I have learned the most wisdom from ...

Someone who has inspired me ...

Autumn reminds me of those who have guided me ...

Date: / /

Searching for signs and symbols

Notice where the theme of *ancestors* shows up this week in your dreams, landscape, or imagination. You can invoke your ancestors by creating altars in your home with photographs, heirlooms, candles, and other items that help you feel connected to those who have gone before you. You might also sense your *ancestors* connected to a particular tree, to migrating birds, or even in the flicker of a candle.

Write/draw/doodle about the the ancestor *connections that you find around you.*

How beautifully
the leaves grow old!
How full of light and
color are their last days!

John Burroughs

Embracing mindfulness

Imagine yourself in conversation with a loved one who has crossed over from life to death. What would you like to say to them? You can imagine the conversation in your mind, speak it out loud, or even draft it in this journal. Be open to listening as well as to speaking.

Weekly practice

Through the coming week, pay attention to moments when you see, hear, or experience something that reminds you of an ancestor. Nature may help you recall them when you feel a sudden breeze or hear a bird call. Notice things that inspire favorite memories or connections to those ancestors whose lives continue to guide you.

Weekly theme

Impermanence

Setting intentions

Impermanence reminds us that all things exist for limited time. Everything in the world, and in our lives, is constantly changing. Perhaps no other season embodies this reality in the way that autumn does. We experience the fullness of colored leaves' and fruit trees' transition into dormancy.

Write/draw/doodle your hopes and intentions for the week ahead. Imagine how the concept of impermanence might impact you in a positive way. What does it mean that nothing is fixed, that even our challenges are temporary?

Some prompts to spark your reflections

I let go of fixed ideas ...

The challenges in my life will also pass ...

I am open to change ...

Date: / /

Searching for signs and symbols

Notice where the theme of *impermanence* shows up this week in your dreams, landscape, or imagination. Trees embody the cycle of life, death, and renewal, but you may also connect with impermanence through seasonal symbols like skeletons, candles, and butterflies.

Write/draw/doodle about the impermanence *connections that you find around you.*

The leaves are fading and falling,
The winds are rough and wild ...
The roots of the bright red roses
Will keep alive in the snow.

Alice Cary

Embracing mindfulness

There can be deep emotional and spiritual growth in recognizing that the very nature of life is impermanence. This understanding can nurture a greater appreciation for the gifts and beauty of the present moment.

Weekly practice

Mindfulness practice reminds us that our thoughts and emotions are not permanent states. This week, you might explore a meditation practice, noticing how time spent with your breath shifts your emotional state. You might also try a walking meditation outdoors—a practice of mindfully placing one foot in front of the other. Find a quiet trail or path where you can take your time with this practice.

Weekly theme

Gratitude

Setting intentions

Many of the themes we've explored so far about autumn—including harvest, celebration, and impermanence—lead us back to living with gratitude. Living with gratitude means showing an appreciation for all that we have—and offering that sense to others.

Write/draw/doodle your hopes and intentions for the week ahead. Consider gifts, blessings, or relationships that you may have taken for granted. How does your heart open when you recognize and appreciate all that you have, rather than focusing on what you lack?

Some prompts to spark your reflections

I am grateful for ...

I recognize these gifts ...

I can be open to gratitude by ...

Date: / /

Searching for signs and symbols

Notice where the theme of *gratitude* shows up this week in your dreams, landscape, or imagination. Gratitude and grief may seem at odds, but they often coexist. Your dreams—whether asleep or daydreaming—might be a place where grief and gratitude intertwine. Allow space for gratitude that can hold the losses or sadness you may be feeling this season.

Write/draw/doodle about the gratitude *connections that you find around you.*

I awoke
this morning
with devout
thanksgiving
for my friends,
the old and the new.

Ralph Waldo Emerson

Embracing mindfulness

Friends include, of course, the humans we love and appreciate. But we can also express gratitude for our non-human companions: the birds that greet you in the morning, the animals who share your home, and even the elements of earth—rocks, stone, and soil—that support your life. Offer words of thanks for all the beings and spirits that surround you.

Weekly practice

Many faith traditions include blessings before eating. These rituals can sometimes become rote. This week, pause before your coffee or tea, your snacks and meals. Think about the farmers who grew your food, the soil and water that nourished it, the truck drivers who transported it, and the workers who placed it on the shelf. Notice how your experience of eating and drinking shifts when you bring mindfulness and gratitude into the act.

Weekly theme

Letting go

Setting intentions

Autumn is a bridge between the summer and winter seasons, linking a time of abundance and light to the darker days when parts of the natural world sleep. Autumn is an ideal time to practice letting go of what no longer serves us as we move closer towards winter days.

Write/draw/doodle your hopes and intentions for the week ahead. Consider anything that feels heavy in your life, that is weighing you down. What would it feel like to let that thing go?

Some prompts to spark your reflections

I am ready to release ...

As autumn arrives, I no longer want to carry ...

It's time to let go of ...

Date: / /

Searching for signs and symbols
Notice where the theme of *letting go* shows up this week in your dreams, landscape, or imagination. Pay attention to the natural world around you—the flowers and trees, branches, seeds, and leaves. What do you observe that symbolizes the idea of release?

Write/draw/doodle about the letting go *connections that you find around you.*

Be like a tree.
Let the dead
leaves drop.

Rumi

Embracing mindfulness

Imagine yourself as a tree in autumn. See what kind of tree you are, what you look like full of leaves and life. Describe the story, from your tree perspective, of letting your leaves fall.

Weekly practice

Through the coming week, notice any resistance that comes up as you practice "letting go." Resistance is natural and part of any change process. Respond to your resistance with compassion—you can even write a letter to your resistance, explaining how letting go is okay.

Weekly theme

Transition

Setting intentions

We feel transitions taking place in autumn. We move from warmer to cooler weather, observe trees dropping their leaves, and watch animals instinctively preparing for the colder season ahead. Autumn offers us a metaphorical period to prepare and transition into the winter season, so we don't arrive at colder, darker days all at once.

Write/draw/doodle your hopes and intentions for the week ahead. Think about things that are shifting or beginning to change in your life. How can you prepare yourself for the season ahead?

Some prompts to spark your reflections

More and more, change feels ...

I can feel the season changing when ...

I am getting ready for winter by ...

Date: / /

Searching for signs and symbols

Notice where the theme of *transition* shows up this week in your dreams, landscape, or imagination. Pay attention to animals and birds; sky, sun, and moon; light and darkness. What is moving from one state to another in the world around you?

Write/draw/doodle about the transition *connections that you find around you.*

Shed no tear!
O shed no tear!
The flower will bloom
another year.

John Keats

Embracing mindfulness

It's natural for humans to feel anxious when changes take place around and inside of us. Take some time to think about the beauty of spring and remember that everything preparing for winter in the natural world will return.

Weekly practice

The winter months are an ideal time for cozy reading, crafting, or other indoor activities. Start making lists of things you'd like to read, watch, or create so you have something to look forward to when winter arrives!

Weekly theme

Dusk

Setting intentions

Dusk occurs when the sunset disappears but it's not fully nighttime yet. It's an in-between time, full of possibilities. Dusk occurs earlier during the autumn months.

Write/draw/doodle your hopes and intentions for the week ahead. Dusk is a gradual process, guiding us from one moment to the next.

Some prompts to spark your reflections

In the dusk hour, I can see ...
As the nights get darker, I can ...
During in-between times, I am able to ...

Date: / /

Searching for signs and symbols

Notice where the theme of *dusk* shows up this week in your dreams, landscape, or imagination. Dusk is a great setting in stories, poetry, and art, representing possibility and transformation.

Write/draw/doodle about the dusk *connections that you find around you.*

Softly the evening came. The sun from the western horizon
Like a magician extended his golden wand o'er the landscape ...

Henry Wadsworth Longfellow

Embracing mindfulness

Spend time experiencing the dusk hour without artificial light and see what emerges. Notice the difference between sunset and dusk, and between dusk and nightfall—and how your body and spirit experience the changes in light.

Weekly practice

Through the coming week, notice how the increase in darkness affects your mood and energy. If it causes fatigue, low energy, or sadness, get outdoors during the daytime to absorb the positive effects of sunlight. Try bringing more candles or other lights into your living space. What other things could you add to your environment to help with a cozy transition to winter?

Weekly theme

Transformation

Setting intentions

An external transformation is a dramatic change in outward appearance; think of the metamorphosis of caterpillar to butterfly. Our inner transformations may be less visible—but no less dramatic. The landscape transforms through the autumn season, inviting us to notice similar changes in our inner world.

Write/draw/doodle your hopes and intentions for the week ahead. Think about the changes you sense happening inside of you—ways you have grown, shifted perspective, or opened up to something new.

Some prompts to spark your reflections

I witness the way I ...

More and more, I see the world ...

I no longer have to ...

Date: / /

Searching for signs and symbols

Notice where the theme of *transformation* shows up this week in your dreams, landscape, or imagination. Mythology is full of transformation stories, from ancient legends to superhero stories. Myths capture the way humans go through profound changes in inner and outer power.

Write/draw/doodle about the transformation *connections that you find around you.*

Just when the caterpillar thought the world was over, it became a butterfly.

Proverb

Embracing mindfulness

Think about which stage you find yourself in now: caterpillar, butterfly, or the chrysalis stage in between them. Use those metaphors to explore the kinds of changes and transformations happening inside and outside of you.

Weekly practice

Sometimes when we transform, we disrupt old patterns and relationships. Not everyone will recognize, appreciate, or honor the ways we've changed. This week, give yourself the recognition you deserve and do something special to honor your autumn transformations. When recognition comes from within, it carries the deepest power.

Autumn reflections

When we pay attention to seasonal transitions, they can become powerful gateways to new adventures and opportunities. Take a moment to reflect on the harvest, balance, gratitude, and transformations that you have experienced this autumn. You may also want to acknowledge any challenges or grief that shaped these past months. Write down the insights and wisdom you've gathered—gifts that can enrich your life as you step into winter.

Make this reflection page as interactive and personal as you like! You might paste in a ticket stub from a favorite play, concert, or harvest event; a note from someone special; a photo or two; even a fallen leaf.

Some prompts to spark your reflections

Favorite people I shared time with ...

Beautiful places I experienced ...

New and enjoyable activities ...

Times when I felt vibrant, connected, alive ...

All that I hope to release ...

Wisdom I'm carrying into the new season ...

Notes

Published in 2026 by Smith Street Books
Naarm (Melbourne) | Australia
smithstreetbooks.com

Distributed outside of ANZ, North & Latin America by
Thames & Hudson Ltd., 6–24 Britannia Street, London, WC1X 9JD
thamesandhudson.com

EU Authorised Representative: Interart S.A.R.L.
19 rue Charles Auray, 93500 Pantin, Paris, France
productsafety@thameshudson.co.uk; www.interart.fr

ISBN: 978-1-9235-0320-5

Smith Street Books respectfully acknowledges the Wurundjeri People of the Kulin Nation, who are the Traditional Owners of the land on which we work, and we pay our respects to their Elders past and present.

Publisher: Hannah Koelmeyer
Editor: Helen Koehne
Design, layout and illustrations: Silvia Virgillo • puntuale
Proofreader: Pamela Dunne
Production manager: Aisling Coughlan

Printed & bound in China by C&C Offset Printing Co., Ltd.

Book 470
10 9 8 7 6 5 4 3 2 1

FSC www.fsc.org MIX Paper | Supporting responsible forestry FSC® C008047